JARROLD SHORT WALKS
leisure walks for all ages

Snowdonia

Compiled by
Terry Marsh

W0006298

JARROLD
publishing

Mapping sourced from Ordnance Survey

Text: Terry Marsh
Photography: Terry Marsh
Editor: James Hopkin
Designer: Sarah Crouch

© Jarrold Publishing 2003

 This product
includes mapping
data licensed from Ordnance Survey®
with the permission of the Controller of
Her Majesty's Stationery Office.
© Crown Copyright 2002. All rights
reserved. Licence number
100017593. Ordnance Survey, the OS
symbol and Pathfinder are registered
trademarks and Explorer, Landranger
and Outdoor Leisure are trademarks of
the Ordnance Survey, the national
mapping agency of Great Britain.

Jarrold Publishing ISBN 0-7117-2422-9

While every care has been taken to
ensure the accuracy of the route
directions, the publishers cannot
accept responsibility for errors or
omissions, or for changes in details
given. The countryside is not static:
hedges and fences can be removed,
field boundaries can alter, footpaths
can be rerouted and changes in
ownership can result in the closure or
diversion of some concessionary
paths. Also, paths that are easy and
pleasant for walking in fine conditions
may become slippery, muddy and
difficult in wet weather, while stepping-
stones across rivers and streams may
become impassable.

If you find an inaccuracy in either the
text or maps, please write or e-mail to
Jarrold Publishing at one of the
addresses below.

First published 2003
by Jarrold Publishing

Printed in Belgium
by Proost NV, Turnhout. 1/03

Jarrold Publishing
Pathfinder Guides, Whitefriars,
Norwich NR3 1TR
E-mail: pathfinder@jarrold.com
www.jarrold-publishing.co.uk

Front cover: Tryfan in winter
Previous page: Beddgelert

Contents

SCALE 1:312 500 or 1 INCH to 5 MILES *1CM to 3.1 KM*

0   2   4   6   8   10 KILOMETRES   15

0   2   4   6   MILES   8   10

KEYMAP HEIGHTS SHOWN IN FEET

Keymap 2

SCALE 1:312 500 or 1 INCH to 5 MILES *1CM to 3.1 KM*

0   2   4   6   8   10 KILOMETRES   15

0   2   4   6   MILES   8   10

KEYMAP HEIGHTS SHOWN IN FEET

CARDIGAN BAY /
BAE CEREDIGION

Introduction

The routes and information in this book have been devised specifically with families and children in mind. All the walks include points of interest as well as a question to provide an objective.

If you, or your children, have not walked before, choose from the shorter walks for your first outings, although only one of the walks is especially demanding. The purpose is not simply to get from A to B, but to enjoy an exploration, which may be just a steady stroll in the countryside, alongside rivers and lakes, or at the edge of mountains.

The walks are graded by length and difficulty, but few landscapes are truly flat, something of a rarity in Snowdonia, so even short walks may involve some ascent, although nowhere is this excessive. Details are given under Route Features in the first information box for each route. But the precise nature of the ground underfoot will depend on recent weather conditions. If you do set out on a walk and discover the going is harder than you expected, or the weather has deteriorated, do not be afraid to turn back. The route will always be there another day, when you are fitter or the children are more experienced or the weather is better. Almost all the walks involve some measure of rough terrain or steep grassy slopes, making it advisable to wear proper walking footwear rather than trainers or wellington boots. Some are not suitable for cloudy days.

Bear in mind that the countryside changes. Landmarks may disappear, gates may becomes stiles, rights-of-way may be altered. In a few places the terrain can be confusing, and this means having to pay rather close attention to route descriptions and waymarking or, in the absence of waymarking, the general direction followed by the path.

A few of the walks venture into truly mountainous terrain, at a low level, but it seems strange to produce a book, even of short walks, without paying a visit to the top of Snowdon. To make life easier, this walk makes use of the Snowdon Mountain Railway to reach the highest summit in England and Wales, leaving you simply to walk down to Llanberis.

Snowdonia

Generally, though incorrectly, only the mountain ranges which are found in the extreme north-west of Wales are known by the name Snowdonia – Eryri in the old Welsh language. In fact, Snowdonia, in the guise of a National Park, covers a much larger area of over 827 square miles (2,142 square kilometres) and extends far south to Bala and beyond: this book does the same, and tries walks in all parts of the National Park.

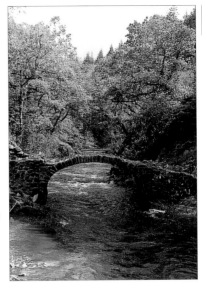

Stone bridge, Afon Mawddach

Anyone venturing into the bosom of Snowdonia soon finds themselves among mountains that have an affinity with higher ranges elsewhere in Britain and the world. And although much of the countryside in the valleys is beautiful, fecund and green, the terrain above the intake walls is often rugged and broken, a place where rocks predominate and the level of difficulty begins a few notches higher than a pastoral walk in Oxfordshire or the Chiltern Hills.

Here there really is something for everyone, from charming green valleys and mature woodlands to craggy topknots and fast-flowing rivers. There is, too, a rich legacy of an industrial past from lead mines to gold mines, and a history of evil spirits and troubled times to rival any part of Britain.

But this is a place to be respected and admired, not feared. A landscape to be loved, enjoyed and shared. Above all else, this is a place where you can learn what it is that appeals to so many regular walkers not only in Wales but throughout Britain.

1 *Llyn Geirionydd*

START Trefriw
DISTANCE 2 miles (3km)
TIME 1 hour
PARKING Car park at Llyn Geirionydd (Pay and Display)
ROUTE FEATURES Woodland, tree roots, slippery rocks, lakeside paths

This is a lovely and straightforward walk, passing through an area of great tranquillity and of no little importance to those who study the history of Welsh poetry. Gwydyr Forest is massive (20,000 acres/8,000 hectares) and comprises huge stands of Sitka spruce, Japanese larch, lodgepole pine and Douglas fir. Its great expanse today covers a vast area of lead mining, which still has dangerous shafts, so it is important not to stray from the paths.

Leave the car park and turn left along the road, but take the first turning on the right, at a barrier, onto a broad track (waymarked). The path touches upon the end of the lake, an area favoured in springtime by marsh marigold, lady's smock and bog myrtle, the latter, if crushed and rubbed onto the skin is an effective deterrent to summertime midges.

As the track bends left Ⓐ near a stone cottage, leave it by turning right over a step-stile, to gain a path that sets off for the lakeshore, passing first across a cleared pasture before running below lakeside woodland.

The Forest Commission's work at **Llyn Geirionydd** began in 1929 and now imbues the place with an air of tranquillity, softening the effects of the intensive mining of the 1870s. The waste tip on which the car park stands and the adjacent mine levels were part of the New Pandora mine complex. Lead ore was delivered by tramway along the eastern shore of the lake, then by aerial ropeway to the Klondike lead mill and mine 200ft (60m) below.

PUBLIC TRANSPORT None
PUBLIC TOILETS At start
ORDNANCE SURVEY MAP Explorer OL17 (Snowdon & Conwy Valley), Landranger 115 (Snowdon)

0 1 KM
HALF MILE

Take care passing along the lakeside path as you cross slippery tree roots and rocks, but keep an eye open for common sandpipers and the occasional grey heron which favour this remote lake and rock habitat.

> **?** Can you discover who or what the monument at the end of the lake commemorates?

About two-thirds of the way down the lake the path seems to come to an abrupt end at a rocky point. But backtrack a few strides to find that

Primroses on banks at Llyn Geirionydd

Llyn Geirionydd WALK 1 **11**

it actually scrambles easily across a rocky shoulder, descending a little awkwardly on the other side to reach a fenced area of old mine workings. Here the path touches the lakeshore, before pressing on once more into the edge of the woodland.

The path eventually reaches a ladder-stile beyond which it keeps to the right of a low wall and leads up to a low building standing beside a rough track.

Off to the left is a monument topped by a cross, to which a short diversion is well worthwhile because it gives a lovely view back along the length of the lake.

Follow the rough track out across the lake end to a metal kissing-gate giving onto the forest road. Turn right, and follow the road back alongside the lake to reach the starting point. Ignore any branching paths.

Woodland path above Llyn Geirionydd

● White–water cascades ● woodland wildlife ● wild flowers

Torrent Walk

START Brithdir
DISTANCE 2 miles (3km)
TIME 1 hour
PARKING Lay-by on B4416
ROUTE FEATURES Woodland trails, steps, gated road

2

The 'torrent' in question is the Afon Clywedog, which here bullies a way through a narrow ravine, losing 300ft (91m) of height in the process. The result is a spectacularly turbulent river section that assaults eyes and ears as readily as the woodland garlic scents the springtime air.

From the roadside lay-by (not far from a school) walk south along the road for the short distance to a signposted path on the right.

Go through a gate and descend to cross a footbridge spanning the river. Beyond, a clear path leads downhill, never far from the turbulence. But take care, the path has many rocky steps and these can be slippery when wet.

The journey down to the foot of the torrent is delightful all the way,

The **Torrent Walk** was created by Thomas Payne who was commissioned by Baron Richards, Chief Baron of the Exchequer, to build an extension to the gardens of his mansion at Caerynwch. Originally, the path used both banks of the river, but one side has become overgrown and unsafe.

sheltered by mature beech trees, and offering many opportunities to view the torrent.

Ⓐ Eventually the path leads out to a quiet road. Turn right, crossing a bridge, and almost immediately

PUBLIC TRANSPORT Buses along B4416
REFRESHMENTS Dolgellau
PUBLIC TOILETS None on route
ORDNANCE SURVEY MAP Explorer OL23 (Cadair Idris & Llyn Tegid), Landranger 124 (Dolgellau)

branch right
onto a narrow, rising
lane. A little more distant
from the river, this nevertheless
provides good views of it.

Steadily, the road (which is gated)
climbs through pleasant woodland
to meet the B4416, and here you
turn right for the short walk back
to the lay-by.   ●

*The woodland area and
the falls are popular with
grey wagtails – a grey
and yellow bird with
a long tail which it wags
incessantly. See
if you can spot any.*

The Afon Clywedog

Afon Llugwy and the Miners' Bridge

START Betws-y-coed
DISTANCE 2¼ miles (3.8km)
TIME 1 hour
PARKING Car park at Betws station (Pay and Display)
ROUTE FEATURES Woodland trails and paths, riverside paths, forest road

3

This simple walk is delightful every step of the way, but you need to be careful about some of those steps because there are many slippery rocks and tree roots to contend with. The Afon Llugwy ('afon' being the Welsh for 'river') is a busy river, bustling its way down from the mountains near Capel Curig, and barging through the narrow gorge which features at the turning point of this walk.

Begin from the main car park in Betws-y-coed (though there is another near Pont-y-pair which can be used, shortening the walk a little) and walk towards the telephone box and toilets, there turning right onto a paved path across and then around a playing field.

When the path rejoins the main road, keep forward on a roadside path above the river. Keep an eye open for the darting flight of grey wagtails that love this habitat.

At the turning for Trefriw, **A** leave the main road, crossing the bridge, with lovely views either side of the turbulent river. Take the first left after the bridge, and then almost

? *Can you discover in which year Dulwich College was evacuated to this area?*

PUBLIC TRANSPORT Bus and rail services to Betws-y-coed
REFRESHMENTS Café at station and along A5
PICNIC/PLAY AREA Near start and at Pont-y-pair
PUBLIC TOILETS At start and at Pont-y-pair
ORDNANCE SURVEY MAP Explorer OL17 (Snowdon & Conwy Valley), Landranger 115 (Snowdon)

0 _____ 1 KM
HALF MILE

immediately branch left, near a picnic area, onto a riverside path.

Head upstream through mixed woodland of pine, hazel, oak, rhododendron and holly. In early summer the woodland is carpeted with bluebells, which bring an intense colour to the scene.

The Afon Llugwy at Betws-y-coed

Bluebells alongside the Afon Llugwy

The path never strays far from the river, and needs a little care as it crosses tree roots and slippery rocks. It leads round a rocky knoll to a ladder-stile at the water's edge, giving into a large cleared area. Cross this, keeping to the footpath, and reach another ladder-stile on the far side.

Beyond the stile, you return to woodland, where the path shortly climbs a little to pass around an old mine, and soon arrives at the oddly shaped Miners' Bridge **B**.

Don't cross the bridge, but turn away, onto a signposted path that climbs steeply but briefly into the

> The mines here were never massively productive, and are now all closed and lost in the undergrowth. **Miners' Bridge** was constructed to shorten the journey the miners had to make, and it provides a spectacular view of the river, as it forces a way through a narrow rocky gorge.

woodland above the river. The path is not waymarked, but is clear as it ascends to meet a surfaced forest road.

Turn right onto the road. When it forks, keep right, and follow the forest road back to Pont-y-pair and from there back to the start. ●

4 *Llyn Barfog*

START Minor road between Cwrt and Tywyn
DISTANCE 2 miles (3.5km)
TIME 1 hour
PARKING Car park in Happy Valley (National Park)
ROUTE FEATURES farm tracks, upland paths, stiles, old mine workings

The fine ridge of hills north of the Dyfi conceal a beautiful lake nestling among the rock outcrops. Known as Llyn Barfog, which means 'the bearded lake', it is thought that the name comes from the lush growth of water-lilies that spread across the surface of the lake during the summer months.

The walk begins at a National Park car park in the appropriately named Happy Valley, a dale of verdant beauty. Walk to the far end of the car park and go through a metal kissing-gate onto a farm track. Turn left towards the farm.

Happy Valley has long been popular with tourists since the railways brought Victorian holiday-makers to the resorts of Aberdyfi. It was at this time that the name 'Happy Valley' supplanted the original Cwm Dyffryn.

On reaching the farmhouse (Tyddyn-y-briddell), go left on a broad track to a high ladder-stile and then continue with the on-going track, which shortly starts to climb energetically.

After another stile, beside a gate, the gradient eases as the track crosses upland pasture. When it forks, bear right, to a gate beyond which a narrow path descends gently to the shores of Llyn Barfog, nestling neatly in a craggy hollow Ⓐ.

PUBLIC TRANSPORT None
REFRESHMENTS None
PUBLIC TOILETS None on route
ORDNANCE SURVEY MAP Explorer OL23 (Cadair Idris & Llyn Tegid), Landranger 135 (Aberystwyth)

According to legend, fairies used to pasture their cattle around **Llyn Barfog**. A farmer who contrived to capture one of their cows was blessed with good fortune until in time the cow was sent for slaughter. As the butcher's knife fell, a fairy called the cow home: the cow, its calves and the fairy all vanished, along with the farmer's luck.

The path continues past the lake, but this is not your direction, though a walk down to the shores of the lake is quite in order. A short distance after the gate you will see a gap on the right passing through the low ridge of hills. This is the way to go, following a path that soon widens into a grassy track and runs on to meet another Ⓑ as the Dyfi Estuary and the hills of northern Ceredigion come into view.

Bear right to a stile and continue on the track beyond, following it in delightfully airy fashion as it skims along a hill shoulder and, after another stile, bears right to descend to an isolated cottage Ⓒ.

Keep to the right of the cottage (ignoring all other signposted routes), and then follow a rough track that soon begins to descend very steeply.

Happy Valley

Young children should be closely supervised here not only because of the gradient but also because the area is one where lead was mined and there are still some open shafts to be found.

Carn March Arthur

Llyn Barfog ('the bearded lake')

Follow the track down to rejoin the outward route near Tyddyn-y-briddell Farm. There, turn left over a ladder-stile to pass the farm and retrace your steps to the car park.

> **?** Can you find the hoofprint of King Arthur's horse?

Castell y Bere

START Llanfihangel-y-pennant
DISTANCE 2 miles (3.2km)
TIME 1 hour
PARKING Castell y Bere
ROUTE FEATURES Field paths and tracks (very muddy), narrow lanes, stiles

Set in a beautiful and fertile valley, this easy walk is both delightful and full of interest. The main focal point is Castell y Bere, stronghold of the last native Welsh prince, but there is, also, a poignant tale of Christian endeavour.

There is a small car park at the entrance to Castell y Bere, and from it walk back along the road for about 300 yds (273m), as far as a path signpost on the right. Cross a stile and go forward across the ensuing field, passing around the edge of Castell y Bere.

Castell y Bere is a native Welsh castle built in 1221 by Llywelyn the Great to secure the southern border of the mountainous stronghold of Gwynedd. From the castle, which is freely open to visitors and well worth a visit, there is a splendid view down the valley to Bird Rock (Craig yr Aderyn), once at the sea's edge and still a breeding ground for cormorants.

The Afon Gamlan, Ganllwyd

PUBLIC TRANSPORT Buses to Abergynolwyn
REFRESHMENTS Pubs in Abergynolwyn
PUBLIC TOILETS None on route
ORDNANCE SURVEY MAP Explorer OL23 (Cadair Idris & Llyn Tegid), Landranger 135 (Aberystwyth)

Once beyond the end of the rocky outcrop that supports the ancient castle, keep forward along a fenceline to a ladder-stile.

Over the stile, turn immediately right and follow a fenceline towards a farm. At the far end of the field, go through a gate onto a farm access track, and bear left through the farm.

Near the farmhouse **A**, turn left through a gate and across the muddy end of a pasture to reach a concrete bridge spanning the Afon Cadair.

After the bridge, turn right through a gate and walk alongside the river for a while, crossing a couple of ladder-stiles and some very wet ground.

At the second stile, turn onto a gravel track going past a cottage **B** and walk out to meet a surfaced lane.

As you join the surfaced lane, you do so at a monument on the site of the home **(Tyn-y-ddol)** of Mary Jones, a young lass who, in 1800, walked barefoot to Bala to procure a Welsh bible for which she had saved for over six years. Sadly, the Rev Thomas Charles had sold the last bible, but he was so impressed with Mary's determination that he gave her his own, an event that was to inspire the formation of the British and Foreign Bible Society.

St Michael's Church, Llanfihangel

Turn right and walk down the road to visit the church **C** at Llanfihangel-y-pennant.

Monument Tyn-y-ddol

St Michael's Church is a 19th-century restoration of a much earlier church, probably 12th century. In the vestry is the full story of Mary Jones, and the Bro Dysynny Map. The Bro Dysynny Map is a three-dimensional model of the valley, (14 miles long and 4 miles wide), from the heights of Cadair Idris to Cardigan Bay. The details of the landscape are worked in embroidered fabric made by 18 people of all ages and both sexes, who live in the area.

Continue past the church and walk along the road to return to the start.

●

 When was the Bro Dysynny Map made?

6 *Coed Ganllwyd*

START Ganllwyd
DISTANCE 2½ miles (4km)
TIME 1½ hours
PARKING Car park at Ganllwyd
ROUTE FEATURES Woodland paths, upland trails, ladder stiles, slippery rocks

This brief walk from the village of Ganllwyd features some spectacular cascades and an impressive waterfall, all set in beautiful mixed woodland. Above it all, the lower slopes of Y Garn were a source of Welsh gold for many years, and the walk pays a visit to the remains of the mine buildings.

Leave the car park and cross the road to a narrow lane (signposted to Rhaeadr Du) ascending through a gate alongside the Afon Gamlan, which throughout its length provides exciting vistas of white-water cascades.

The lane is flanked by rowan, oak, hawthorn and beech, and when it forks, branch left, climbing steadily.

As the lane bears right, leave it by turning onto a rough path heading for a nearby waymark. From the waymark go left on a descending path to a footbridge spanning the river **Ⓐ**.

Just before the bridge, high up on the right, is a slate tablet (erected in 1973 and now showing signs of weathering) containing a poem by **Thomas Gray** from his 'Ode to the Deity of the Grande Chartreuse'. The original, now illegible and carved in an adjacent rock, is thought to have been done by the owner, W A Maddocks, of nearby Dolmelynllyn (now a hotel).

PUBLIC TRANSPORT Buses to Ganllwyd
REFRESHMENTS Dolgellau
PUBLIC TOILETS At start
ORDNANCE SURVEY MAP Explorer OL18 (Harlech, Portmadog & Bala), Landranger 124 (Dolgellau)

Cross the footbridge and turn right on a stony path (very slippery underfoot) that climbs to the spectacular double falls of Rhaeadr Du (*you will need to control young children here*).

The path climbs above the falls to a waymark, and here, turn left, up through the trees, soon to walk alongside a moss-covered wall.

Eventually, the path reaches another waymark close by a ladder-stile spanning a wall. Ignore the waymark and cross the stile **B**, then follow a narrow path through young, mixed woodland of birch, spruce and rhododendron with many of the trees encroaching onto the path and likely to give you a good soaking after rain.

? *See if you can find a young 'Christmas' tree growing in the woodland*

Continue to meet a broad forest track. Cross the track, and keep forward once more on a waymarked path of gravel ascending through pine trees.

The path presses on beside a low, moss-covered wall and a stream, and shortly touches on another forest trail at a bend. Ignore the trail, but keep ahead onto a waymarked track. A short way farther on leave the track at a waymarked stile of curious construction. Cross the ensuing wooden bridge and bear right on a 'stepping stone' path to reach a higher track near old mine buildings.

Turn left and pass the dilapidated barracks where the miners lived, and soon reach a high (and rickety) ladder-stile crossing a wall ⊙. Over this, go down a grassy path through bracken (taking care if the grass is wet) following a waymarked route.

Shortly, pass through a dilapidated wall and head (boggily) for another ladder-stile. Over the stile, cross a stream and go towards a ruined barn, keeping to the left of it and

Old field barn, Ganllwyd

Coed Ganllwyd

descending to reach a step-stile near a gate.

Cross a narrow surfaced lane, and head down a track to a footbridge and gate. Through the gate, turn right, descending initially beside a wall (and ignoring a path going left). Keep descending through agreeable woodland until the path reaches a low waymark near a fence and gate. Go forward through the gate, still descending, with the path soon running alongside the wall.

When the wall changes direction, go half-right to a gap, now with the Afon Gamlan on your left. Through the gap walk down to another gap near a building beyond which you soon reach the road. Turn left to return to the start a short distance away. ●

Aber Falls

START Aber
DISTANCE 2¾ miles (4.5km)
TIME 1½–2 hours
PARKING Car park at Bont Newydd
ROUTE FEATURES Riverside paths, woodland trails, stiles

7

The Aber Falls (Rhaeadr-fawr) has long been a popular walk with visitors to North Wales. In recent years the path to the falls has been hugely improved and is now an easy walk. This route, however, makes an alternative approach through a pine plantation before returning along the main valley route.

Begin from the parking area near Bont Newydd, an attractive single-arch bridge spanning the Afon Rhaeadr-fawr (there is a Pay and Display car park over the bridge and a short way along the road. It isn't necessary to start and finish at Bont Newydd, but the riverside path makes it worthwhile to do so).

Aber, or to give it its full name **Abergwyngregyn** (the River Mouth of the White Shells), was the place where Llywelyn ap Iorwerth, called 'Llywelyn the Great', had a palace, a favourite spot with the Princes of Gwynedd.

Turn in through a gate beside the bridge and follow a lovely riverside path through woodland. Keep an eye open for dippers and grey wagtails, as well as buzzards overhead.

The path leads to a wooden footbridge spanning the river, beyond which it leads to a gate giving onto the main track up the valley. Turn right.

When the ongoing track forks, branch right. The track continues up the valley, but just before

PUBLIC TRANSPORT Buses to Aber village
REFRESHMENTS Pub in Aber
PUBLIC TOILETS None on route
ORDNANCE SURVEY MAP Explorer OL17 (Snowdon & Conwy Valley), Landranger 115 (Snowdon)

This lovely valley has a mosaic of woodlands with a variety of bark-loving lichens and mosses and a cross-section of woodland and mountain birds like **ring ouzel**, **wheatear** and **raven**. It has been occupied since the Bronze Age.

reaching a cottage, keep an eye open for a path branching on the left (signposted) and offering a way to the waterfalls through the valley plantation.

A Initially, the path runs along the plantation edge, but at a stile enters the plantation. On the way, this route affords a lovely view of the Aber Falls and the slightly lesser falls (Rhaeadr-bach), to their right, both set in a wild cwm at the valley head, beyond which rise the domed and craggy summits of the northern Carneddau.

The path runs along an avenue of trees, mainly pine, all of which seem to lean rather drunkenly to the left.

At the end of the plantation, cross another ladder-stile and immediately bear right onto a descending path heading for the foot of the falls.

The path leads down to yet another stile, beyond which the waterfalls, to the left, are easily reached. *Young children will need close supervision among the rocks at the base of the falls.*

Having visited the falls, and perhaps enjoyed a relaxing picnic, simply turn around and walk back out of the valley, following the main path.

In the valley you will find some recording equipment. What is it recording?

On the way out, the track passes **Nant Rhaeadr,** a typical Welsh *tyddyn* or smallholding, which kept a few cows, sheep and the occasional goat. The farmer used all the land available to him: the garden for herbs and vegetables, the mountain pastures for grazing, and the forest for firewood and making tools. Nant Rhaeadr was a popular spot with Victorian tourists, and was something of a wayside café, selling tea and home-made lemonade.

Continue out of the valley, shortly rejoining the outward route which, just before a gate, bears left to cross the footbridge spanning the valley river and return through the woodland walked at the start of the walk.

The main track to Aber Falls

8 *Bala Lake*

START Llangower
DISTANCE 3½ miles
(5.8km)
TIME 2 hours
PARKING Car park at Bala
lakehead
ROUTE FEATURES
Woodland trails, farm
paths, roads

This walk takes advantage of the narrow-gauge Bala Lake Railway that operates during summer months along the southern shore of Llyn Tegid. Using the train to reach Llangower and then walking back over the hillsides south of the lake, there are stunning views of the surrounding countryside and Bala's place in it.

Begin from a car park a short way north of the Llangower turning, and walk along the edge of the lake and over a lovely triple-arched bridge to reach the station. This top end of the lake has some fine willow scrub, popular with reed bunting and the rather noisy (but usually unseen) sedge warbler.

Take the train to Llangower, and leave the station there, turning left along the road towards the village with its pretty churchyard. Go past the churchyard, over a roadbridge, and continue to the next road turning on the right.

The trackbed of the **Bala Lake Railway** was once part of the old Great Western Railway line between Ruabon and Barmouth, closed in 1965 as uneconomical. Today's trains only operate between April and September, every day in July and August, but during other months excluding Mondays and Fridays. Information about train times is available by ringing 01678 540666 or connecting to www.bala-lake-railway.co.uk.

Climb steadily for about 400 yds (364m), as far as a farm track doubling back on the left (footpath signpost) **A**. Turn onto this,

---

PUBLIC TRANSPORT Buses to Bala and lake railway station
REFRESHMENTS Bala
PUBLIC TOILETS Bala and Llangower
ORDNANCE SURVEY MAP Explorer OL23 (Cadair Idris & Llyn Tegid),
Landranger 125 (Bala & Lake Vyrnwy)

Bala Lake Railway

climbing gently with a good view forward to the mountainous area north of Bala.

The track descends briefly to pass a farm and then climbs again. As the track bears left towards a large house, leave it at a signpost (waymark) going forward on a grassy track, passing to the right of the house, and then going through a gate on the other side. Beyond the gate, bear left to another giving into the edge of woodland.

Now follow a path along the bottom edge of a wooded slope graced by some ancient beech trees. Part way along the slope, near what looks like an old quarry, go through a wooden gate and continue alongside a post and wire, with a lovely distant view of Bala at the head of the lake.

Once the highpoint of the path is reached, so the descent is leisurely, initially beside another fence.

In this wooded area, in spring and early summer you will find the lovely white flowers of wood sorrel, which favour the shaded habitat provided by trees and have leaves rather like **clover**. Keep a lookout for **bluebells**, too.

A short way further look for a waymark on a tree, at a stream crossing **B**. Here branch left, descending steeply beside the stream. There is no path here, and finding the ongoing route requires some careful observation, spotting yellow arrow waymarks. *Take care, too, on the descent, especially if the grass is wet.*

After about 150 yds (136m), you need to cross the stream. There is a yellow waymark on a tree on the other side of the stream, but it is not easy to spot. From it you descend half-right to a ladder-stile, the top of which you can see below, at the edge of another streambed.

Over the stile, cross a shallow ford and then another ladder-stile, continuing beyond alongside a fence marking the boundary of broad-leaved woodland. At the end of the woodland, the path forks. Take the right branch which climbs across a bracken slope, rising steadily as a grassy path to a ladder-stile on the skyline above.

Churchyard, Llangower

Over this, turn left onto a descending bridleway, going down until you reach another stile. Cross this and walk down to intercept a surfaced lane **C**.

Now follow the lane down to meet the valley road, and there turn right, taking care against approaching traffic (the road is generally quiet but can be busy in summer months). If you timed your walk correctly you should be treated to a close-up view of the steam train.

? *In summer months the hill slopes are frequented by the white-rumped wheatear. See if you can spot any.*

Map labels:

Ysgol / Sch

Ffynnon Beuno

P

HERITAGE CENTRE

Weir

Lake Wardens Office

P

PC

Pont Mwnwgl-y-llyn

Motte & Bailey

Sailing Club

Pen-

Ffridd Fach-ddeiliog

93

Bala Lake Hotel

Ty'n-y-bryn

92

Graienyn

Y Coed

Wenallt

Bryniau Bach

34

Llyn Tegid / Bala Lake

Bala Lake Railway Rheilffordd Llyn Tegid

177

Beudy Graienyn

Ffridd Goed

Ffridd Uchaf

Cefn-ddwygraig

Bryniau Golau

Bryn Hynod Station

175

Bryntirion

Coed Ty'n-y-twll

C

Coed Bryn-hynod

Bryniau Goleu

Cornelau

Beudy Bryn-bedwog

33

Ty'n-y-mûr

Bryn Porfa

172

Bryn-hynod

Sheepfold

Bryn-bedw

B

Coed y Gilwern

Pant-yr-onen

Coed Pant-yr-onen

32

Is-

Creiglau Bychain

A

Coed yr Allt

Weir

Glyn Gower

Fedw Ty-cerig

Glyn-bach

Waterfall

9 *Cwm Idwal*

START Ogwen
DISTANCE 3 miles (4.7km)
TIME 2 hours
PARKING Car park at start (Pay and Display)
ROUTE FEATURES Rough bouldery paths, rocky terrain, ladder stiles

Cwm Idwal, popularly known as the Devil's Kitchen, is a ruggedly splendid introduction to mountain terrain. This walk, although rocky underfoot, is generally straightforward, but climbs on a stepped path through a massive downfall of boulders below the black gash of Twll Du in the valley headwall. This section can be intimidating and tiring, but is not unduly difficult.

Begin from the car park at Ogwen and walk around the buildings onto a rising, rocky path at the rear. This soon leads to a couple of ladder-stiles and a footbridge spanning a tributary stream.

Follow the path until it reaches the shores of Llyn Idwal Ⓐ, a truly dramatic setting. Turn right to cross a double-gated footbridge, and continue on a rough stony path around the northern end of the lake.

Cwm Idwal and the adjacent mountains are designated as a National Nature Reserve for botanical and geological reasons. The landscape was shaped by glaciers during the last Ice Age, which ended about 11,000 years ago, and is regarded as one of the finest examples of glaciated landform in Britain.

When it becomes possible to do so, leave the main path and descend to a pebbly beach at the edge of the lake, and walk across to a gap in a wall.

PUBLIC TRANSPORT Buses to start
REFRESHMENTS Snack bar at start
PUBLIC TOILETS At start
ORDNANCE SURVEY MAP Explorer OL17 (Snowdon & Conwy Valley), Landranger 115 (Snowdon)

Beyond the wall continue on a stony path through glacial moraine, heading towards the cliffs of the valley headwall, in which the black gash of Twll Du is prominent.

> Across this glacial landscape, vegetation includes **heather** and rare **arctic-alpine plants** and has evolved over the past 500 years as a result of upland farming. Please do not pick the plants.

Beyond the end of the lake, a stepped rocky path **B** begins to climb more steeply (the steps can be tiring). If the prospect of continuing does not appeal, simply turn around and retrace the outward route. Otherwise, ascend steadily, pausing frequently to take in the retrospective view of the cwm, beyond which the massive bulk of Pen yr Ole Wen looms impressively.

> **?** The ring ouzel, also known as the mountain blackbird, looks like a blackbird, but has a white bib. See if you can spot any.

Llyn Idwal and Pen yr Ole Wen

Higher up, the path threads a way through a massive downfall of boulders where, from time to time, hands may be needed to maintain balance: it's rather like ants climbing across a bowl of sugar lumps. *Young children will need close attention here.*

Eventually the path levels and passes a rough shelter beneath a boulder **C**, and soon begins to descend as it meets the path coming down from Twll Du.

Here, start going down, taking great care.

The descending path soon breaks free of the boulders, and continues a constructed descent to the foot of a popular rock climbing cliff, the Idwal Slabs.

Continue past the Slabs, following a clear path out of the valley to rejoin the outward route near the gated footbridge. Turn right and return to Ogwen. ●

Llyn Elsi

START Betws-y-coed
DISTANCE 3 miles (4.7km)
TIME 2 hours
PARKING Car park at
Betws station (Pay and
Display)
ROUTE FEATURES
Woodland trails and
paths, lakeside paths

*This delightful forest walk climbs
steadily to a tranquil lake set amid wild
mountains. The route is straightforward
throughout, but some care is needed
towards the end as the path zigzags down
through the forest. Keep eyes and ears
open for woodland wildlife. Take a
picnic to enjoy overlooking the lake.*

From the station walk out to
the main road and cross at a
pedestrian crossing. Turn towards
the church, and take the first
turning on the left, into a side
street that leads round to the back
of the church, from where a broad
track (signposted to Llyn Elsi) sets
off into the woodland.

The route, which ascends steadily,
is waymarked by poles topped with
blue and white paint, and leads
through a beautiful mixed
woodland of oak and sycamore,
giving way higher up to various
members of the 'pine' family.

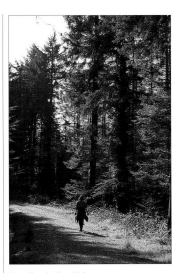

Woodland, Llyn Elsi

PUBLIC TRANSPORT Bus and rail services to Betws-y-coed
REFRESHMENTS Café at station
PUBLIC TOILETS At start
ORDNANCE SURVEY MAP Explorer OL17 (Snowdon & Conwy Valley),
Landranger 115 (Snowdon)

Higher up, the track forks **A**. Take the right branch, now following poles topped only with white paint. Continue following these waymarks through numerous twists and turns, eventually to burst upon the lovely Llyn Elsi, **B** surrounded by trees, but with distant views of Moel Siabod and the northern hills of Snowdonia.

Having reached the lake, turn right on a branching path leading to a memorial erected in commemoration of the opening of the 'Bettws y Coed Waterworks'. This is a splendid vantage point, and a nearby bench makes it a suitable place for a breather or a picnic.

Now walk past the memorial. There are three paths, but take the one with the white-topped poles. This leads through less dense scrub, and shortly crosses a forest trail.

Monument, Llyn Elsi

Llyn Elsi

Continue following the white-topped waymarks, which lead down eventually to another forest trail. This time, turn right to follow the trail, but only as far as a clear path **C** branching left, back into woodland, and continuing to be waymarked by white-topped poles.

Keep an eye open on the way through the woodland for the moss-covered remains of a building on the left. These wooded hillsides would once have been populated, and the isolated buildings used for storage or for living in during the summer months.

The upper part of the plantation has numerous 'pine' trees. These produce seed heads, known as cones, but there are many different sizes. See how many different ones you can find.

The descending path zigzags through the woodland, but finally emerges on the main track used on the ascent, near a signpost. Turn left and retrace the outward route to the starting point of the walk at Betws-y-coed.

11 *Sygun and Llyn Dinas*

START	Beddgelert
DISTANCE	3½ miles (5.8km)
TIME	2–3 hours
PARKING	Near Royal Goat Hotel (Pay and Display)
ROUTE FEATURES	riverside trails, mountain uplands, two significant ascents

This is a walk of two distinct halves: the first easy, the second much more demanding across mountain upland. Anyone reluctant to engage the climbs can simply return from Llyn Dinas. Two uphill sections are involved, along with one awkward moment at Bwlch-y-Sygyn, followed by some slithery downhill sections through rhododendron bushes. The views are excellent throughout.

Beginning from the car park near the Royal Goat Hotel, walk out to the road and turn left towards the bridge spanning the Afon Colwyn. Before the bridge, turn right onto a lane parallel with the river (signposted to Gelert's Grave).

At the turning for Gelert's Grave, keep forward over Glaslyn Bridge, and on the other side bear left to pass the left-hand edge of a row of terrace cottages.

Cross a road near a bridge and go forward onto the Riverside Walk, passing through gates to enter an area heavily populated with rhododendron and gorse.

The riverside path ends at a ladder-stile giving onto a surfaced lane. Keep ahead, and at the end of the lane, go through a gate and towards the Sygun Copper Mine.

Continue as far as the entrance to the mine Ⓐ and there turn left

PUBLIC TRANSPORT Buses to Beddgelert
REFRESHMENTS Pubs and cafés in Beddgelert
PUBLIC TOILETS In Beddgelert, alongside river
ORDNANCE SURVEY MAP Explorer OL17 (Snowdon & Conwy Valley), Landranger 115 (Snowdon)

onto a broad track leading out towards the road. Go as far as a bridge spanning the river.

> The place by the river is the site of **'dressing' sheds** used as part of the copper mine. Dressing involved the separation of copper ore from waste by crushing the rock before sieving it in water.

Immediately before the bridge, bear right onto a signposted path heading up river. A delightful path now leads up towards Llyn Dinas.

> Beyond the river and across the road is a small hillock, **Dinas Emrys,** from which Llyn Dinas takes its name. This was a small fort, occupied during the Early Iron Age until the Dark Ages.

When the path reaches a footbridge, ignore it and keep forward to a kissing-gate giving onto the shores of Llyn Dinas, a lovely place for a picnic **B**. Here, through the gate, immediately turn right onto a clear ascending path up the hillside above.

At this point the nature of the walk changes and becomes more rugged. It is a good introduction to mountainous terrain, but not suitable for very young children as it involves a moment or two at the top of the second climb where hands (and bottoms) will be needed to aid progress. Anyone not happy with this prospect should simply retrace the outward route to Beddgelert and, perhaps, combine it with a visit to the copper mine.

Beddgelert

The path climbs energetically for a while before finally taking leave of Llyn Dinas and looking forward as it crosses a stretch of mountain moorland where tough heather and bracken dominate the landscape.

A middle section that is level, leads to another uphill stretch, as the path climbs to a signposted junction **C**. Keep forward at this point (for Beddgelert) and immediately pass through a small mining area with ruined buildings and mine entrances in the hillside that should not be explored.

Continue up to cross a ladder-stile at Bwlch-y-Sygyn, from where a fine viewpoint embraces Moel Hebog, Moel Lefn and Moel yr Ogof and the distant Nantlle Ridge.

Now, at the very start of the descent, comes an awkward moment as the path goes down a rock step. This is a brief interlude and easy enough to deal with (in reverse if necessary), but for a few moments it calls for increased care and attention. *Children will need careful supervision here.*

> **?** *See if you can discover where the Glaslyn Foundry is.*

Heading for Llyn Dinas

The ongoing path soon becomes grassy, and just as it starts to descend for a second time look for a branching path on the left, leading up to a signpost, and then continue for Beddgelert.

The path now follows the crest of a heathery ridge, with wild mountain moorland off to the left. Keep going as far as a large cairn on a rock outcrop, and here, at a path junction, bear right, descending.

More care is needed now throughout the remaining descent.

The path threads a way through stands of rhododendron, is rocky in places and elsewhere grassy. It leads to a metal kissing-gate in a wall, beyond which it continues as a grassy track.

In among the rhododendron the going is often muddy and slippery. Nor is the path as distinct as it might be and a bit of casting about may be necessary to find the driest line. All routes lead steadily downwards to the path used on the outward route. When this is reached, turn left beside the river, and retrace the outward route to Beddgelert.

●

12 *Llyn Gwernan*

START Ty-nant, near Dolgellau

DISTANCE 3½ miles (5.5km)

TIME 2 hours

PARKING Car park at Ty-nant

ROUTE FEATURES lakeside paths, ancient road, stiles, farm tracks, some uphill

This walk visits an area of Snowdonia better known for its high mountains than its peaceful tracks. But the walled track that is the middle part of the walk crosses delightful countryside with constantly changing views and a strange sense of remoteness.

From the car park, walk towards the toilets and go through a farm gate, bearing immediately right after a stream onto a broad track, but leaving it straight away to follow an indistinct path initially alongside the stream, then following a wall to a ladder-stile.

Beyond the stile, stay parallel with a wall, doing your best to avoid muddy ground and boulders – there is no distinct path here, but you can follow an intermittent line of waymark poles across a pasture.

Behind you **Cadair Idris** and its acolytes loom large, filling the southern horizon. The distinctive feature of the range derives from the way ice has gouged great corrie basins into the volcanic rocks with impressive results, producing a huge scale of erosion that is in itself fascinating. For over 50 years, Robin Edwards of Dolgellau guided clients across these mountains, a practice that continued into the early 20th century.

On the far side of the field, the path improves for a while as it enters the next pasture, once more heading

PUBLIC TRANSPORT Only to Dolgellau

REFRESHMENTS Gwernan Lake Hotel

PUBLIC TOILETS At start

ORDNANCE SURVEY MAP Explorer OL23 (Cadair Idris & Llyn Tegid), Landranger 124 (Dolgellau)

Llyn Gwernan

for a ladder-stile in a wall corner. Over the stile the path follows a boggy course through tussock grass and willow scrub, squelching to an end at another stile.

Beyond, more scrub awaits, but in summer the place is loud with the voices of warblers – wood and willow, chiffchaff and blackcap.

Gradually the path improves as it enters an area of pine trees just as it reaches the edge of Llyn Gwernan. Another stile gives onto a lovely lakeside path now followed leisurely.

Just as you are beginning to enjoy the lakeside path, it veers away into the cover of young woodland, and shortly heads into a pine plantation, from which it escapes at a ladder-stile giving onto a green track alongside a fence.

Go forward towards a ruined building **Ⓐ**, and as you reach the ruin, turn left, and climb steeply on a grassy path, not initially very clear, but parallel with a wall. The path rises to a metal gate, from which it continues briefly along the boundary of mixed woodland.

Ruined farm buildings, Llyn Gwernan

Soon the path bears away and passes round (or over) a low hill to a stile beside a gate. Beyond this it encounters a stunning, enclosed ancient track **B**, probably an old drove road, that now strikes forward across an upland region that few (I suspect) visit.

With no opportunity to vary the route, the walled track heads roughly south-west for a mile (1.6km), offering views north to the Rhinogs and, later, south to Cadair Idris.

The walled path finally ends at a gate near a stone barn. Cross a small enclosure to a narrow metal gate, then look for a low waymark a short distance ahead, directing the path right through a wall gap, after which it goes through another nearby wall gap, and turns left.

> **?** *Along the walled track only one tree appears. Can you discover what kind it is?*

Now descend steeply on a farm vehicle track to intercept a wide bridleway **C**. Turn left (waymark on left), facing Cadair Idris. As the track starts to climb and bends left, leave it by walking to a nearby gate (waymark) beyond which the path descends gently into lovely birch woodland, which ends, all too soon, at another gate.

Through the gate, cross a stream and climb steeply right to a wide track above. Turn left, following the track, as, a short way on, it ascends to the right of a wall. At a waymark, leave the wall and climb steeply right to another waymark and a gate above.

Through the gate, go forward on a path enclosed between a wall and fence that leads to Tyddyn-Evan-fychan Farm (where on my visit [May 2002] the dogs were loud and aggressive). Go past the farm, and walk out along its access to return to the start. ●

Nearby **Dolgellau** is an ancient market town. Roman roads meet here and, in 1404, Owain Glyndwr (a descendant through his mother of the last native Prince of Wales), assembled the last Welsh Parliament, from which he appointed ambassadors to go to France to sign a treaty of alliance with Charles IV against the English.

13 *Coed-y-Brenin*

START Ganllwyd

DISTANCE 3½ miles (5.5km)

TIME 2 hours

PARKING Tyddyn Gwladys Picnic Site

ROUTE FEATURES Broad woodland tracks, footbridges, road walking

This beautifully simple walk travels the two banks of the Afon Mawddach deep within the confines of the Coed-y-Brenin Forest. Always turbulent, the river produces an impressive display of force, as does its neighbour, the Afon Cain. Both meet up near the site of a gold mine, where the diligent and patient might still find a grain or two.

Leave the picnic site by turning right onto the surfaced forest road, which soon degenerates into a stony track and leads past the holiday cottages at Ferndale.

Keep on above the narrow gorge containing the Afon Mawddach, passing a number of ruined buildings mostly associated with the lead and gold mines that once operated in this area.

Near the confluence of the Mawddach and the Cain Ⓐ,

Pistyll Cain, Coed-y-Brenin

PUBLIC TRANSPORT Buses to Ganllwyd

REFRESHMENTS Dolgellau

PICNIC AREA At start

PUBLIC TOILETS Ganllwyd

ORDNANCE SURVEY MAP Explorer OL18 (Harlech, Portmadog & Bala), Landranger 124 (Dolgellau)

the track swings right over a bridge. From it a short path deviates left to view Pistyll Cain, a splendid waterfall tucked away in a corner.

Back on the main track, you soon reach the site of the Gwynfynydd Gold Mine Mill, of which only derelict buildings remain.

Gold was first found in **Gwynfynydd** in 1863, but it was not until 1887 that the Welsh 'gold king', William Pritchard Morgan found the first major vein. The mine was closed in 1916, but in the 1930s there was an attempt to re-open the mine, and the mill was rebuilt. This was short-lived, as the mill burned down in 1935 before it became fully operational. The mine is now largely underground (for environmental and security reasons), and in recent years did start producing gold again, though this is now believed to have stopped.

The track climbs past the mill site and a short way on you need to branch right from it to reach a new footbridge, replacing a partially collapsed stone bridge seen just upstream.

Over the bridge, turn right, climbing on a broad track, now going with the flow of the river. The track rises to meet another. Here, turn right, immediately descending.

Panning for gold, Coed-y-Brenin

after a gate and a branching track (on the left) **B**, you can cross the river by another footbridge which offers a lovely view of the Mawddach in its rocky gorge.

Over the bridge go up to join the surfaced forest track and turn right, following this back to the start. On the way back, as throughout the walk, keep eyes and ears open for summertime warblers – wood, willow, chiffchaff and blackcap. ●

When the descending track forks, keep right, always staying alongside the river.

Keep following the forest track for about 1½ miles (2.5km) until, just

? *Can you discover how many mills were used at the Gwynfynydd Gold Mine to process the ore?*

Afon Mawddach, Coed-y-Brenin

Above Penmaenmawr

START Sychnant Pass, Conwy

DISTANCE 4 miles (6.5km)

TIME 2 hours

PARKING Sychnant Pass

ROUTE FEATURES hill tracks and paths, ladder stiles, vehicle tracks

At first glance the minor ridge sandwiched between Conwy Mountain and Tal y Fan seems innocuous enough, but it has considerable prehistory, in the form of hilltop cairns and stone circles, and an invigorating, airy feel about it – a fine walk high above the Conwy Valley.

Begin from the parking area at the top of Sychnant Pass and cross the road to a gate opposite giving onto a broad path leading around a low rock outcrop.

After 200 yds (183m) turn sharply right at a waymark for the North Wales Path, onto a rising path. Using the waymarks as a guide, follow a twisting trail, mostly a grassy path through bracken and heather.

The Path, a moderate-distance walk across North Wales, climbs steadily, and when it forks, near overhead powerlines, keep left.

Huge standing stones dot this landscape, and many of the hills have large cairns on their summits, each with some past significance. Undoubtedly erected by man, they are a clear indication of the importance of this area in prehistoric times.

By continuing simply to follow the waymarked route, the path eventually meets up with the powerlines once more. Go beneath them and bear left, in due course reaching a ladder-stile beside a gate **Ⓐ**.

Beyond the stile, descend a little across the western slopes of Maen

PUBLIC TRANSPORT Bus and rail services to Conwy

REFRESHMENTS Pubs and cafés in Conwy and Dwygyfylchi

PUBLIC TOILETS None on route

ORDNANCE SURVEY MAP Explorer OL17 (Snowdon & Conwy Valley), Landranger 115 (Snowdon)

Mist in Conwy Valley

Esgob, and, at an obvious break in the ridge of low hills on your left, keep right, staying on the North Wales Path.

> ⚐ There is a splendid view westwards to the hills that rise above **Penmaenmawr,** many dotted with cairns, standing stones and more recent farmhouses. These coastal hills have been farmed for thousands of years, and continue to sustain a viable, if arduous, sheep farming economy.

The path soon runs alongside a drystone wall, but then, at another waymark, starts to move away from the wall and passing beneath the powerlines once more, now going forward as a narrow path across a bracken slope.

When the path next forks, bear right towards a small stand of trees surrounding a derelict farmhouse **B**.

Here, take your leave of the North Wales Path, by turning left alongside a wall.

At a nearby wall corner, keep ahead, walking away from the farmhouse, climbing gently.

The ongoing path maintains the same direction as it crosses the main thrust of the low ridge of hills, on the far side reaching a wall, now with a lovely view forward over the Conwy Valley.

Turn left alongside the wall, but later, as it changes direction, move away from the wall by following a broad green path. Before long, however, the path returns to parallel the wall and soon reaches an indistinct stone circle.

Continue past the stone circle, beyond which the track once more temporarily abandons the wall and climbs to cross the shoulder of a

Stone circle, Cefn Llechen

low hill, later linking up with the wall again as the path starts to descend to meet a broad rutted vehicle track.

Follow the track, which comes down to a junction near sheep pens. Here, bear left on another vehicle track, but almost immediately branch left by turning onto a green path heading for a small lake.

Keep to the left of the lake, on a grassy path that pushes a way through bracken to a stile spanning a wall. Over this, follow a clear path, crossing another hill shoulder and then descending to a path junction.

This is a good place to keep an eye open in summer for the darting flight of **stonechats,** and for small groups of wild ponies that roam the hills.

Keep on in the same direction, roughly following the course of a wall, and shortly meeting up with the North Wales Path again, at a waymark, where the outward route is rejoined. Here, branch right and retrace the outward route to return to the top of Sychnant Pass.

Many of the low hilltops are crowned by large cairns, some of which have prehistoric significance. See how many you can count.

15 *Mawddach Estuary*

START	Penmaenpool
DISTANCE	4½ miles (7.4km)
TIME	2–3 hours
PARKING	Penmaenpool
ROUTE FEATURES	estuary, woodland, mountain upland, farmland

Beginning along the shores of the Mawddach Estuary this walk later turns inland to an infrequently visited area of craggy uplands before threading a lovely way down through farmland and forest. The estuary is an excellent place to view waders and gulls, while the hillsides are popular with mountain birds like wheatear, pipits and the occasional ring ouzel.

Walk towards the toll bridge spanning the estuary, cross the road and go forward along the edge of the estuary, passing the George III Hotel. Initially, the track is surfaced, but it soon resorts to the old railway trackbed that ran from Barmouth to Ruabon, opened in 1865 by the Great Western Railway but closed 100 years later.

Go past cottages to a gate giving into a railway cutting, now regenerated with wild flowers, ferns, sycamore, oak and holly.

Keep going along the trackbed beside the estuary and eventually pass Abergwynant Woods on the left.

The **Abergwynant Woods** are one of only two surviving fragments of the woodlands on this side of the estuary that provided oak for the shipbuilding that took place in creeks along the river during the 18th and 19th centuries.

Gradually the trackbed closes in on the estuary until finally it is travelling alongside it, at the

PUBLIC TRANSPORT Buses to Penmaenpool
REFRESHMENTS Penmaenpool
PUBLIC TOILETS At start
ORDNANCE SURVEY MAP Explorer OL23 (Cadair Idris & Llyn Tegid), Landranger 124 (Dolgellau)

Directly across the estuary is the **village of Bontddu** set against hills that were at the centre of a goldrush in the 19th century. Prospectors discovered gold in the area in 1834 while digging for copper. Dolgellau enjoyed a brief boom as prospectors and miners flooded into the area from 1860 to 1902, but by the 1920s, the industry had almost disappeared.

Old Railway station, Penmaenpool

water's edge. Keep an eye open along this stretch for the large black and white shelduck, which has a broad chestnut band around its chest. The ducks are often found on the estuary in pairs or small groups.

Mawddach Estuary, at Penmaenpool

Continue along the trackbed until you reach a bridge spanning the in-flowing Afon Gwynant **Ⓐ**, and there leave the trackbed by branching left onto a broad track alongside the river.

Follow the riverside track into woodland, which is eventually deflected right, through a metal gate (waymark) towards Abergwynant Farm. The track soon rejoins the company of the river, which is usually fast flowing, and leading out to a single-arched bridge near the farm.

Ignore the bridge, and go forward onto a surfaced farm access, which leads attractively up to a road junction. There turn left but immediately leave the road by branching right onto a side road leading to a youth hostel, initially climbing steeply through woodland.

Walk up the road, flanked by bluebells, celandine and Welsh poppies, and pass along the top edge of the river gorge, through which the Gwynant forces a white-water way. Continue as far as the turning to Cae'n-y-coed **B**. Here leave the ascending road and branch left through a metal gate.

When the ensuing farm access forks, branch right to a gate and stile. The on-going track zigzags upwards and eventually climbs to run just below the ridge of Dolgledr, parallel with a wall. The track rises through a lovely craggy landscape of knolls, nooks and crannies, and eventually (after another gate) passes round the end of the wall. But, just before this point, keep an eye open for a yellow waymark locating a stile across the wall **C**. Take this and in the ensuing pasture, go forward on a broad grassy path, soon descending into a shallow valley (waymark).

A narrow path runs through the valley, eventually close by a fence leading down to a ladder-stile. Beyond, a green path accompanies a wall and then goes past a small copse before crossing a tumbledown wall and turning right to another stile.

From the stile bear left on a rough vehicle track. As you approach a corrugated iron-roofed stone barn in a wall corner, keep an eye open for a low waymark pole on the left with the number 7 on it, and from this strike down-field towards a farm.

Go through two gates and then take a track on the left to another ladder-stile and gate from which a rough track runs on. It climbs past a slate-roofed barn (now as a permissive path) and curves right before rejoining the right-of-way at a signpost.

Turn left onto a rough access track, but as this swings right, leave it by going left across a narrow grassy col between two low hills (waymark), and immediately locate a stile giving into cleared woodland.

A path leads down to meet a forest trail. Go left onto this and continue as far as the first cottage on the right. There turn through a narrow gate with a waymark on it. Turn through this and follow a path down to the Penmaenpool road.

At the road, cross with care, and then turn left down towards the George III Hotel, there rejoining the estuary path a short distance from the start. ●

> **The Welsh gold found above the Mawddach Estuary is renowned for its light colour and was traditionally used for a special purpose. Can you discover what that purpose was?**

16 Yr Wyddfa (Snowdon)

START Llanberis
DISTANCE 4¼ miles (7.5km)
TIME 2 hours
PARKING Llanberis
ROUTE FEATURES high mountain paths, steep slopes, loose stones

Although only taken in descent, this visit to the summit of England and Wales is still a tough walk and needs decent footwear and wind- and waterproof clothing. Best reserved for a clear day, this walk provides superb views of the high mountains and Wales, and gives an invigorating sense of freedom.

Take the mountain railway to the summit of Snowdon, enjoying the hour-long steady climb up to the top of the mountain. Once at the top, walk steeply up to the summit cairn and/or visit the nearby café before setting off down.

The descending track initially is very close to the railway, and leads first to a large standing stone Ⓐ from which there is a stupendous view eastwards to Crib Goch, the Glyders, Moel Siabod and the three lakes visited in Walk 19.

Keep on past the standing stone, and soon the on-going path forks. The right branch climbs onto the second highest summit hereabouts, Crib-y-ddysgl, but you should ignore this and keep forward, still following the course of the railway, though this is now dropping away from the path.

The path curves gently around the north-western shoulder of Crib-y-ddysgl and then starts to descend very steeply on loose stones and rocks. *Take great care here.*

PUBLIC TRANSPORT Buses to Llanberis
REFRESHMENTS Llanberis and at Snowdon summit
PUBLIC TOILETS At start and Snowdon summit
ORDNANCE SURVEY MAP Explorer OL17 (Snowdon & Conwy Valley), Landranger 115 (Snowdon)

The idea of a mountain railway on Snowdon was originated early in the 19th century, but it was only with the formation of the **Snowdon Mountain Tramroad and Hotels Company** in 1894 that the possibility came to fruition. There are nine operational locomotives today: five steam and four diesels. The average gradient is 1:7.8 (12.85 per cent) and the steepest is 1:5.5 (18 per cent)

Snowdon Horseshoe

Gradually, the path levels as it runs beside the railway again on the approach to Clogwyn Station. The path passes very close to the rim of Cwm Hetiau **B** (*keep children under close control here*) before swinging left through a tunnel beneath the railway.

Beyond the tunnel, keep forward, descending again and once more on an awkward section of loose rocks. Off to the left you can see the stern dark cliffs of Clogwyn Du'r Arddu, one of the severest climbing 'playgrounds' in Wales.

Clogwyn Du'r Arddu was the scene during the 1950s and 1960s of many early rock climbing routes, then at the highest extreme of climbing. Many were first ascended by the Salford pairing of Don Whillans and Joe Brown, but later climbers have added their own tally of impressive routes to the 'black cliff'. This is not a place for novices.

The Moel Eilio group from the Llanberis Path

> **See how many of the nine locomotives you can spot.**

The path pulls away from the cliffs and continues down, now below the railway until, below Halfway Station, it crosses the track again **C**. The gradient is now much easier as the path continues its descent to meet the end of a surfaced lane at a gate.

Turn right and follow the road steeply downwards and then out down a long street to reach Llanberis near the Victoria Hotel.●

Cwm Bochlwyd and Cwm Tryfan

START Ogwen

DISTANCE 4½ miles (7.3km)

HEIGHT GAIN 1,395 ft (425m)

TIME 3 hours

PARKING Ogwen

ROUTE FEATURES mountain paths and lakes, stream crossing, stiles, rough paths

Offering the most demanding walk in the book, this ascent to Cwm Bochlwyd and across into the neighbouring Cwm Tryfan effectively circles the great peak, Tryfan, which towers above the A5 at Ogwen. This is a rugged but enjoyable walk, requiring suitable footwear and adequate clothing against wind and rain – though it is best not tackled in such conditions. Take plenty of refreshments.

🥾 Begin from the car park at Ogwen and walk around the buildings onto a rising, rocky path at the rear. This soon leads to a couple of ladder-stiles and a footbridge spanning a tributary stream.

Continue with the path until it turns abruptly to the right to head for Cwm Idwal (Walk 9). Here, on the apex of the bend leave the main track by turning onto a less distinct path Ⓐ tracking across upland

pasture towards the conspicuous cliff, Bochlwyd Buttress (look for the elongated letter 'H' formed by cracks on its face).

Falls near Ogwen

PUBLIC TRANSPORT Buses to Ogwen

REFRESHMENTS Ogwen

PUBLIC TOILETS At start

ORDNANCE SURVEY MAP Explorer OL17 (Snowdon & Conwy Valley), Landranger 115 (Snowdon)

As you near Bochlwyd Buttress the path begins to climb steeply. It has been improved in recent years and though steep is a sure and easy way into the cwm (a mountain hollow) above **B**.

> **Cwm Bochlwyd** is a wonderful place to savour the mountain environment. Glyder Fawr looms darkly above you, while shapely Tryfan stands off to the left, an enticing summit, but too complex for the purposes of this book. Within the cwm lies Llyn Bochlwyd, and many a backpacker has spent a peaceful night camped here.

With the lake to your right, you need to cross the outflowing stream, and then follow a clear rocky path that climbs steadily and steeply to a couple of ladder stiles that appear on the skyline above. These mark Bwlch Tryfan **C**, a high mountain pass.

> The path up to and beyond **Bwlch Tryfan** is a section of **the Miners' Track**, which continues towards the mines below Snowdon. This is the way workers who lived in Bethesda would walk each week to and from their workplace on the other side of the mountain.

Over the stiles, keep forward, looking for a clear path descending into the great hollow that now appears ahead. This is Cwm Tryfan, and a good if rough path runs down its length. A couple of false starts do lead into the path, and it is a question of taking the one you feel most comfortable with, although none is especially

Cwm Bochlwyd

difficult if
treated with
respect. The
original line of
descent begins some way
along the path from Bwlch Tryfan.

Head down the path, below the
steep cliffs of Tryfan across the
face of which you can detect the
rising gash of the Heather
Terrace, an access path onto
the East Face for climbers.

Once beyond Tryfan, the path
heads down to a large rock slab
known as Little Tryfan (Tryfan
Bach) **D**, a practice ground for
novice rock climbers, though even
here all the paraphernalia of rock
climbing is needed.

Keep descending past Little Tryfan
to reach Gwern Gof Uchaf Farm,
and there turn left to walk out
to reach the A5. Turn left and
walk alongside the road back to
Ogwen.   ●

> **?** *The most common bird
> along this walk is the
> meadow pipit: a small
> brown bird with white
> outer tail feathers. See
> if you can spot any.*

18 *Llyn Padarn*

START Llanberis
DISTANCE 5 miles (8km)
TIME 3 hours
PARKING Roadside car park adjoining lake
ROUTE FEATURES Slate quarries, woodland trails, lakeside paths, quiet roads

No visitor to Llanberis can fail to be impressed by the massive example of human endeavour that is portrayed in the slate quarries, a major industry in North Wales for decades. The lake is the larger of two filling the valley (the other is Llyn Peris), and its circuit is a delightful walk with outstanding views of the mountains that form the Snowdon massif.

Leave the lakeside parking area and walk towards the near end of the lake. A footbridge, adjacent to a play and picnic area, gives into another car park. Keep left, following the lake edge and soon enter the Padarn Country Park at a gate.

Go forward on a grassy track to a metal kissing-gate in a fence. Maintain the same direction across the next field, and eventually reach a footbridge spanning the watery link between the two lakes.

Dolbadarn Castle can be seen at the edge of Llyn Peris. It is thought to have been built by Llywelyn the Great, whose grandson, Llywelyn the Last, kept his brother Owain Goch prisoner here. The castle's stunning profile was a great favourite with artists, such as Turner.

The footbridge leads to the Welsh Slate Museum Ⓐ, and here, bear left, following the boundary of the museum towards the terminus for the Lakeside Railway.

PUBLIC TRANSPORT Buses to Llanberis
REFRESHMENTS Cafés/pubs in Llanberis, at Slate Museum and Cwm Derwen Visitor Centre
PLAY AREA Adjoining lake, near start
PUBLIC TOILETS Llanberis
ORDNANCE SURVEY MAP Explorer OL17 (Snowdon & Conwy Valley), Landranger 115 (Snowdon)

Keep to the right of the Lake Railway buildings to locate a woodland path that leads to the V2 Incline.

The V2 Incline, a product of the slate quarrying era, is the only incline working today in the UK. A series of inclined tracks climbs the flanks of the Vivian Quarry, and is a marvel of ingenuity and engineering. The Incline was restored in 1998.

Go past the Incline into woodland, soon climbing on a rocky path and passing numerous trees that are heavy with moss, to meet a surfaced road. Bear left here, but within a few strides branch left onto a path alongside a low wall until steps lead back up to the road at the Quarry Hospital.

Go left, passing the hospital mortuary, to re-enter woodland for what is the finest section of the walk, and follow a path across a wooded slope above Llyn Padarn. Keep an eye open for woodland birds here – nuthatch, jays, chiffchaff, willow warbler.

At a red-topped waymark pole, remain on the woodland path climbing gently with a lovely view across the lake to Llanberis, the rounded dome of Moel Eilio and, further left, the conical summit of Yr Wyddfa (Snowdon).

Llyn Padarn, Llanberis

? *Can you discover anything that tells you when the slate quarrying was at its most active?*

The path climbs quite high above the lake, with steep drops on the left necessitating close supervision of young children. At the high point there is a splendid view up the length of Llyn Padarn.

From here the path starts to drop steeply. When it forks, branch right, following the path to a gate near a series of low cascades embowered with birch and oak **B**.

At the gate, turn right, leaving the Padarn Country Park, and soon cross a slate bridge. Go ahead, now climbing again, on a stony track.

As the rising track levels, it passes a quarry on the right and soon reaches the Cwm Derwen Woodlands and Wildlife Centre (where refreshments are seasonally available).

A little distance beyond the centre the ongoing track is surfaced with concrete. As the track bends right, leave it on the apex, and go left along a narrow path to a kissing-gate giving onto a road near a telephone box. Turn left.

Now simply follow the road through the linear hamlet of Fachwen, steadily descending towards the end of Llyn Padarn. Follow the road out to a T-junction, and there turn left to cross an attractive triple-arched bridge. Over the bridge, bear left to a ladder-stile giving onto an old road along the lake edge.

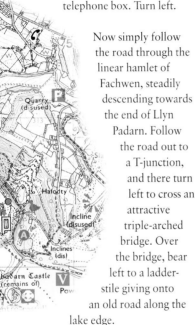

At the third ladder-stile, turn left onto the main valley road and walk along the roadside footpath for 450 yds (410m), as far as a waymarked gap **C** on the left through which a path descends to the trackbed of the railway that formerly ran through the valley as far as Llanberis.

Bear left along the trackbed, taking time to check the lake for great crested grebe and goosander. Keep following the trackbed to a metal barrier (toilets nearby), and here, with a road running ahead, bear left (as if going into the car park) and then immediately right onto another wooded path parallel with the road. This path leads into the edge of another car park.

Keep on in the same direction, picking up the continuing path, and soon emerge onto the road. Go left and walk out towards the main road. Another left turn soon brings the end of the walk at the Village Car Park.   ●

Old bridge at head of Llyn Padarn

19 *The Miners' Track*

START Pen-y-pass
DISTANCE 5½ miles (9km)
HEIGHT GAIN 850 ft
(260m)
TIME 2½ hours
PARKING Pen-y-pass
(Fee charged)
ROUTE FEATURES
mountain tracks, lakes,
high mountains, mine
buildings

This is a linear walk, completed in both directions, using the old track that the miners built to reach the copper mines below Snowdon. Today it is one of the most popular ways to ascend Snowdon, but this walk only goes as far as the top lake, Glaslyn, before turning round to head back for Pen-y-pass.

The walk begins along the broad track clearly heading away from the car park at Pen-y-pass. This is a well-graded track and was originally used to bring copper down from the mines.

The track soon passes the first of three lakes encountered on the walk, Llyn Teyrn **A**.

PUBLIC TRANSPORT Sherpa Bus Service from Nant Peris
REFRESHMENTS Pen-y-pass
PUBLIC TOILETS At start
ORDNANCE SURVEY MAP Explorer OL17 (Snowdon & Conwy Valley),
Landranger 115 (Snowdon)

Llyn Teyrn, the Lake of Ruler, occupies a shallow hollow scooped out by a glacier and is thought to have been named after a local prince. On its shores are the ruins of barracks used by the miners. Local legend has it that the barracks were occupied by French miners escaping the Napoleonic Wars.

As the track continues, so Y Lliwedd, a twin-peaked summit, appears on the left, its steep cliffs the preserve of rock gymnasts and goats. Continue, to turn a corner and discover the largest lake, Llyn Llydaw (Britanny Lake) **B**, at the far end of which the distinctive cone of Snowdon rises dramatically.

Snowdon and Llyn Teyrn

Because of the monster in Glaslyn it is said that no bird will fly completely across the lake, and will always divert away. See if you can spot any that do.

Llyn Llydaw is divided by a causeway constructed during the 19th century, which was once much lower than the present causeway and given to frequent flooding. This necessitated a detour around the lake or the option of getting very wet.

As you cross the causeway, the great red wall of Crib Goch towers above, a spectacular traverse on which many a head for heights has been put to the test. Once over the causeway, keep following the track as it follows the shore of Llyn Llydaw for a while, and then reaches a group of old mine buildings, the main site of industrial activity in the area.

Beyond the mine buildings, the track begins to climb quite steeply, and finally reaches another lake, Glaslyn **C**, its waters tinted remarkably by copper ore.

Glaslyn was once known as Llyn y Ffynnon Las, the **Lake of the Green Fountain,** and is said to be inhabited by a monster, an *afanc*, which once lived in a pool near Betws-y-coed, but caused such havoc among the local population that they carted it by oxen to the lake below Snowdon's gaze.

Glaslyn has a pebble 'beach' and this makes a lovely place to have a mountain picnic before simply retracing your steps to Pen-y-pass.●

Llyn Llydaw from Glaslyn. Moel Siabod in the distance

Conwy Mountain

START Conwy town centre
DISTANCE 5¾ miles (9.4km)
HEIGHT GAIN 885 ft (270m)
TIME 3 hours
PARKING Car parks in town centre (Pay and Display)
ROUTE FEATURES Estuary, stiles, exposed hill top, muddy fields, some road walking

Conwy Mountain provides a grandstand view of Conwy Bay, Great Orme and the eastern summits of the Snowdonia National Park. The walk begins in Conwy, the ancient stronghold of Edward I, where his castle dominates the estuary, and climbs energetically to the top of the mountain, which is topped by an ancient hill fort.

 Leave Conwy by heading onto the quayside. Turn left and shortly pass the Smallest House in Great Britain.

Continue along the quay and out through the town wall. At a road junction bear right onto the signposted North Wales Path. This becomes a pleasant surfaced path leading along the water's edge.

Follow the path to its end, at a road junction Ⓐ, and there turn left and walk out to meet the A547, near a pedestrian crossing. Cross into the road opposite and go over a pedestrian bridge spanning the North Wales railway line. On the other side, continue along a walled track to a surfaced lane and then a road junction.

At the junction, turn right, climbing gently past houses. When the rising track levels and then forks, branch right to a ladder stile giving onto Conwy Mountain.

> **?** *See if you can find a postman on horseback.*

PUBLIC TRANSPORT Rail and bus services to Conwy
REFRESHMENTS Numerous cafés in Conwy
PUBLIC TOILETS On quayside
ORDNANCE SURVEY MAP Explorer OL17 (Snowdon & Conwy Valley), Landranger 115 (Snowdon)

Approaching the summit of Conwy Mountain

The ongoing path climbs through bracken and is flanked by young beech and gorse. It climbs vigorously for a while with improving views south and east that embrace Conwy Castle and the Denbigh hills beyond.

Conwy Castle was one of a chain of seventeen fortresses built by Edward I along the coast of North Wales. Castle and town were built at the same time: the castle affording protection for the town and its people, who in turn looked after the castle. Settlers came, attracted by the shrewd offer of generous conditions for trade, building and leasing. In Edward's time only the English were allowed to live within the town walls, or to run a business. The Welsh had to live outside, and could only pursue occupations as farmers or shepherds.

Ⓑ At a waymark pole, leave the North Wales Path by branching right to intercept a wide grassy path that runs along the spine of the mountain.

Turn left onto this and continue climbing easily. As much as possible following the path along the crest. From time to time paths appear right and left, all of which lead in the same direction, but these do not cross the top of the mountain, which involves a slight detour. Keep an eye open for feral ponies that live along the mountain.

Conwy Castle and Estuary from Conwy Mountain

The top of **Conwy Mountain** is occupied by an ancient hill fort (Castell Caer Seion). This is a pre-Roman Iron Age settlement, which covers a good section of the mountain top.

Continue along the top of the mountain, still following the crest path as it gradually begins to descend to thread a way through low hills at the western end of the ridge, steadily moving to the landward side of the mountain.

The path comes down to meet a broad track **C** at a waymark (once more following the North Wales Path). Keep forward across the track to engage another short ascent before the Path drops to a ford and stepping stones not far south-east of Pen-pyra Farm.

Cross the farm access and either go forward onto a broad grassy track across a low shoulder, or simply turn left along the access track. Both routes rejoin on the other side of the shoulder, from where the track can be followed out to the road at the top of the Sychnant Pass.

D Cross the road and climb to a gate in a wall, beyond which a gently rising path runs beside a wall.

Just as the path passes beneath overhead powerlines it forks. Branch left, onto a narrow path climbing across a hill shoulder and still parallel with a wall.

Soon the path descends to a ladder-stile in a wall corner. Over this, go forward towards a small group of lakes (Gwern Engen), and keep on in the same direction to intercept another rough track. Turn right to a track junction near a group of buildings.

Now bear left and soon descend steeply on a rough track that leads to a narrow road.

Turn right, going past Ty Coch Farm. At the next house on the left (Y Bwthyn), leave the road by turning through an ornate metal kissing-gate onto an enclosed path. The path breaks out at another gate into a field. Strike across this, towards a vehicle track.

Cross the track and go through a wooden gate, and then follow an obvious route across fields linked by gates, finally targeting an oak tree in the third field. The tree stands in a fence corner not far from a small wooded hill that in springtime is bright with primroses.

Aim for a red-roofed black-and-white house, to the right of which another gate gives onto a lane.

E Turn right, following the lane past Oakwood Park Hall to a T-junction. Turn right, and twenty yards further on go left at a signposted path. Now go forward across fields to reach a metal kissing-gate.

Through the gate, bear left along the field edge to meet the Sychnant Pass Road. Turn right and follow the road back towards Conwy.

On reaching the town walls, keep right to pass through a pedestrian archway, then rejoin the main road and walk towards the town centre. At a T-junction, turn right and follow the road through the centre of Conwy towards the castle and the start. ●

Hill fort on the summit of Conwy Mountain

Further Information

Walking Safety

Always take with you both warm and waterproof clothing and sufficient food and drink. Wear suitable footwear, i.e. strong walking boots or shoes that give a good grip over stony ground, on slippery slopes and in muddy conditions. Try to obtain a local weather forecast and bear it in mind before you start. Do not be afraid to abandon your proposed route and return to your starting point in the event of a sudden and unexpected deteriorationin the weather.

All the walks described in this book will be safe to do, given due care

Llyn Gwernan and Tyrau Mawr

and respect, even during the winter. Indeed, a crisp, fine winter day often provides perfect walking conditions, with firm ground underfoot and a clarity of light unique to that time of the year.

The most difficult hazard likely to be encountered is mud, especially when walking along woodland and field paths, farm tracks and bridleways - the latter in particular can often get churned up by cyclists and horses. In summer, an additional difficulty may be narrow and overgrown paths, particularly along the edges of cultivated fields. Neither should constitute a major problem provided that the appropriate footwear is worn.

Follow the Country Code

- Enjoy the countryside and respect its life and work
- Guard against all risk of fire
- Take your litter home
- Fasten all gates
- Help to keep all water clean
- Keep your dogs under control
- Protect wildlife, plants and trees
- Keep to public paths across farmland
- Take special care on country roads

En route to Llyn Dinas

- Leave livestock, crops and machinery alone
- Make no unnecessary noise
- Use gates and stiles to cross fences, hedges and walls

(The Countryside Agency)

Useful Organisations

Snowdonia National Park Office
Penrhyndeudraeth, Gwynedd
LL48 6LF. Tel: 01766 770274
Fax: 01766 771211
Email:parceryri@compuserve.com

CADW: Welsh Historic Monuments
National Assembly for Wales,
Cathays Park, Cardiff CF10 3NQ.
Tel: 029 2050 0200

Fax: 029 2082 6375
Email: cadw@wales.gsi.gov.uk.

Coed Cymru,
The Old Sawmill, Tregynon,
Newtown, Powys SY16 3PL.
Tel: 01686 650777
Fax: 01686 650696
Email: coedcymru@mid-wales.net;
Website: www.coedcymru.mid-wales.net.

Council for the Protection of Rural Wales
Ty Gwyn, 31 High Street,
Welshpool, Powys SY21 7YD.
Tel: 01938 552525
Fax: 01938 552741
Email: yvcw@aol.com.

Countryside Council for Wales
Maes y Ffynnon, Penrhosgarnedd,
Bangor, Gwynedd.
Tel: 01248 385500
Fax: 01248 355782

**National Trust Office for
Wales (North)**
Trinity Square, Llandudno,
Gwynedd LL30 2DE.
Tel: 01492 860123
Fax: 01492 860233

North Wales Wildlife Trust
376 High Street, Bangor,
Gwynedd. Tel: 01248 351541

Ordnance Survey
Romsey Road, Maybush,
Southampton SO16 4GU.
Tel: 023 8030 5030 (Business),
08456 05 05 05 (Public)
Fax: 02380 792615
Email: custinfo@ordsvy.gov.uk;
Website:
www.ordnancesurvey.gov.uk.

Ramblers' Association
2nd Floor, Camelford House,
87-90 Albert Embankment,
London SE1 7TW.
Tel: 020 7339 8585
Fax: 020 7339 8501
Website: www.ramblers.org.uk.

Craig y Bere

Royal Society for the Protection of Birds (RSPB)
The Lodge, Sandy,Beds SG19 2DL.
Tel: 01767 680551
Fax: 01767 692365
Website: www.rspb.org.uk

Tourist Information
Aberdyfi: 01654 767321
Bala: 01678 521021
Barmouth: 01341 280787
Betws-y-coed: 01690 710426
Fax: 01690 710665
Conwy: 01492 592248
Fax: 01492 584376
Corris: 01654 761244
Dolgellau: 01341 422888
Fax: 01341 422576
Llanberis: 01286 870765
Fax: 01286 872141

Travel Information
Bus Traveline
0870 608 2 608
National Rail Enquires
08457 48 49 50
(www.thetrainline.com)

Ordnance Survey Maps of Snowdonia
Outdoor Leisure map (Snowdonia)
Explorer maps OL17 (Snowdon & Conwy valley), OL18 (Harlech, Portmadog & Bala) and OL23 (Cadair Idris & Llyn Tegid), Landranger maps 115 (Snowdon), 124 (Dolgellau), 135 (Aberystwyth) and 125 (Bala & Lake Vyrnwy).

Answers to Questions
Walk 1: It was erected to mark the reputed birthplace on the shores of Llyn Geirionydd of Taliesin the chief bard of the 6th-century, a contemporary, it is said, of the Wizard Merlin.
Walk 2: The grey wagtail is almost always found near water. They like to perch on rocks in the streams, and it is usually their wagging tail that catches the eye.
Walk 3: A plaque near the road junction on the return part of the walk explains that Dulwich College Plot was planted during evacuation to the area in 1941.
Walk 4: Carn March Arthur, above the Dyfi Estuary, is a rock imprinted, it is said, with the hoofprint of the horse that carried King Arthur to safety by leaping across the Dyfi Estuary as he was pursued by enemies. It is marked by a slate standing stone and stands beside the track.
Walk 5: Between October 1992 and July 1995. The information is found in the church.
Walk 6: Above the falls and over the ladder-stile, the mixed woodland contains many young trees of the kind popularly used at Christmas.

Walk 7: The weather.

Walk 8: Wheatear are summer visitors from Africa. The females arrive first: they are buff coloured; then the males arrive. Males are slaty blue in colour.

Walk 9: The ring ouzel frequents rocky terrain like Cwm Idwal, but is difficult to spot. Look for them among the boulders below Twll Du.

Walk 10: There are different species of spruce here, as well as lodgepole pine. Each has a different cone.

Walk 11: Glaslyn Bridge in Beddgelert was built in 1951 at the Glaslyn Foundry in Portmadog.

Walk 12: Holly. Wherever you find holly trees like this along ancient tracks, it lends support to the suggestion that this may have been a drove road, since the tree provided a rough form of feed for cattle.

Walk 13: 40. The information is contained on a panel near the mill site.

Walk 14: There are at least seven, but it sometimes seems like there are more because the same hill is viewed from a different angle.

Walk 15: The gold was used to fashion Royal wedding rings. The information is on a panel alongside the estuary.

Walk 16: Only at busy times are all nine likely to be in use. Four of the steam locomotives were built in 1985/96, and one in 1922.

Walk 17: Meadow pipits are almost as abundant in the mountains as they are in meadows, and are often found in association with the summer visiting wheatears.

Walk 18: 1875-1930s. At the V2 Incline, an information panel reads: 'The incline was used from 1875 until the early 1930s, during the peak of slate production around Llanberis.

Walk 19: Everything depends on whether you believe legends, or the fact that birds seldom fly in a straight line!

Walk 20: There is one on the letterbox built into the wall of Boat House, just outside Conwy town wall.